Hymnswitch

Also by Ali Blythe
Twoism

Ali Blythe

HYMNSWITCH

icehouse poetry
an imprint of Goose Lane Editions

Edited by Phil Hall.
Cover and page design by Julie Scriver.
Printed in Canada by Coach House Printing.
10 9 8 7 6 5 4 3 2 1

Library and Archives Canada Cataloguing in Publication

Blythe, Ali, 1976-, author
Hymnswitch / Ali Blythe.

Poems.
ISBN 978-1-77310-070-8 (softcover)

I. Title.

PS8603.L98H96 2019 C811'.6 C2018-904643-0.

Goose Lane Editions acknowledges the generous financial support of the Government of Canada, the Canada Council for the Arts, and the Province of New Brunswick.

Goose Lane Editions
500 Beaverbrook Court, Suite 330
Fredericton, New Brunswick
CANADA E3B 5X4
www.gooselane.com

Contents

Waking in the Preceding

Hello, My Forever Ago, don't worry,
you won't be reading this much longer.

You will have already returned
in a snowcloud, which is suggestively,

fashionably, only ever one second old.
Yes, darling, it's me, it says

as proof that in space,
though there are many silences,

fleeting isn't the opposite
of *infinite*, but its perfect match.

Let's light a longer candle
with a candle-end

while we drift in the old ways
like these Jovian diffusions.

It causes shivers up and down
the once two-thing

we say goodbye to
when we slowly undress

into the wonderful softness
of our own gendery animalia.

Though not wishing to answer
anything that thrusts too readily

toward a subject, I was once
helped to never again use

"I" when
"I" is not my first person.

Everything permutes
faster than you can imagine.

I remember your body gathering
at the door

I regard daily
as part of my reality

of starving
on flowers and realism.

But in this blindness
we will no longer surveil,

we will no longer widely steer
toward avoidance, we will become

happy, satisfied and uplifted
communications professionals,

back-of-office sunbeams
setting covers aglow.

Contained,
not constrained, by the past.

Childhood I might enter
if I could confiscate adult sadness.

Adulthood I might enter
if I could confiscate childhood sadness.

Outside this weather,
the hare sharply dodges the dog then lifts

over the answer
to reveal the question.

Are we the physics of our dreams?
The ones that keep using

risk erotically.
That isn't said quite right.

But I think you're with me.
It's in the movement.

*

Unmanageability Harmonica

Today I wish to say
something beautiful
but all I have is,

Good morning sixty-three-day
headache, I trust you.
We are for repetition.

Like when the old man
in The Program
talks about the futility

of fixing his hot rod
because it all ends up
in the junkyard

and I say to him,
Way to go, you did a good,
impermanent job.

My only job is to hold
this glass with something
poured into it

other than myself
and think about how
exactly this minute

can save my life again.
You need an edge, a poet
I loved problematically

said when we were both alive.
He also said Johnny Cash
walked straight into the sunset

and it never went down.
I wish you could see
all the good, solid boots

in this circle. Boots
whose owners help me
just because they too

have found themselves
in this room that is a thousand
degrees too warm

to get help in repetitive ways
for what seems to be
largely due

to either painful
or more painful
cultural circumstances.

But when it's my turn
to speak in a new tone
of acceptance

and camaraderie
that sounds in my ears
like the finest, saddest

harmonica,
I'm chicken.
I talk about everything

but the moment I knew
we were no longer friends.
The sun was setting.

There was a bowl of keys
at the door and I had to pick
the right one fast

or the getaway car
wouldn't start.
Or she'd climb in after me.

And even that moment
I don't talk about — the one
that began the year

of drinking
to beat all years,
the getting sober,

finally — I made up.
The sun was rising.
It was all done

and I was driving fast
on the twisty road
out of the woods.

But she was already
in the car. She was using
the windows

of my cinematic getaway
to puke up her mouthfuls
of feather. Tonight,

I will again take off
my red, plaid recovery shirt
and hang it over the lamp

on the bedside table.
I will pull the chain to illume
the Canadian lampshade

in lieu of my chest.
If you just keep walking
into the sun,

it won't ever set.
But here's my little headache,
to say it does.

The Program

The weather is stolen fans.
The time, perpetual 4:30s.
Passing through customs
requires four steps:

a phone call, an intake,
thirty days of the worst clarity
of your life, another intake,
and you're in. I never dreamt this,

but the closest childhood dream
would be the one where you
can't stop shitting yourself
then wake to find it all true.

The small, careful graffiti
in the Men/Trans Men Welcome
john: *For a good time,*
go somewhere else.

The *o* in S.O.B.E.R.
instructs us to Observe:
the gripping hand,
the stinging forearm.

We take notes on triggers.
Someone says,
The desire to erase oneself,
and I wake up

two days later
confirming my chest,
my head,
I didn't blow it.

We aren't so much for news.
We compose children's stories:
"The Anthropomorphized Substance."
"The Father Who Stole My Teeth."

I don't see many dresses.
No lovers allowed.
I concentrate on boots.
Boots, boots, eyes, boots.

Although I notice Griffin
has a griffin tattoo.
I have always thought of *myth*
as its own mythical creature.

Like the four types of stress
reactions on the whiteboard:
Freeze, *Fight*, *Flee* and Freeze's
monstrous relation, *Dissociate*.

If I look the guys around the room
in the eyes — which I'm doing
more of — I can see what reaction
they would like to use right now.

All involve several cigarettes
on break in the sunshine.
We do fierce inventories.
Even though we don't belong

to the AA team.
We belong to Ovid.
He said it took thirty-six hounds
to devour their beloved hunter

who turned stag
when a naked woman
sprinkled his hair
with vengefulness.

Dogs cling to our altered faces.
There is no place left to wound.
We want to say, *Oh, look at me!*
but no voice follows.

Then it's time to go, but where?
If we walk one minute down
the alley we find the relapsed.
At the border, the dead.

There is no leaving sober.
I fear that, like everything,
I'm making this up. Letters from here
are unsendable, of course.

My Animal Family

She wears the bruises
she gave me
around her own neck.

I don't have any
love for you anymore,
we say to each other

in this order:
she goes first
and I never say a thing.

Instead I open my jacket
to show her the animal family.
They attempt feats of daily living.

Owl's motionless soup spoon.
The endless knotted pull
of fox's used handkerchiefs.

Why do you always do that,
she asks,
make it about someone else?

Anesthesiologist

My childhood lake
adjusts its blue gown,
lifts its mask and says,
Count backward from ten.

I peel off my clothes,
then skin, then light,
until I hit nothing.
Should I go into negatives? I ask.

I'm told to just count up.
There's no end to that.
I will count until I surface.
But what a funny timeline.

Yet Why Not Say What Happened?

Of all the 81,941,760 videos
available on YouTube this instant,
we watch one about
the four phases of addiction:

Introductory
Maintenance
Disenchantment
Disaster

Dis means asunder
and *aster* means star.
In this phase, you may
find yourself in risky situations

such as lying in a bed
in the woods
trying to hug someone you love
so they don't kill you.

She almost did, with weapons
that resembled things I also love
like words and hands.
This is where, we are told,

we must get out
or slip from ourselves.
I had no ravishing
animal poem to help me then.

Cups

I invent a parlour game
that pairs Ovid's rapists
to the raped.

Every play must end
in a comforting outcome.
The feathery uprush

of the boy in the eagle's
wings brought forever
to pour out

his wine and beauty
for the gods, perched
there in his clouds,

perhaps wondering
if he himself
ever gets to drink.

Vessel of Bottom Smashed Off

If a woman who thinks they are a man
is mad, a man who thinks they are a man

is no less so, says Nelson,
via Lacan.

The man slams the door.
A reverberation of unmet need.

The man is preceded by his substances
of use, the who-said-what-to-who.

The man's hands are shaking
out masculinity, femininity in the air

— a woman fell from the man
as he stood to leave.

The man should be working.
He's working. Blinking out

and waking up
on a silver and green recovery chair.

He took my glass to the fountain,
tried to fill it to drink. Tried to fill it

and drink. Wet footsteps lead
back to the chair.

The man's chest is numb. Something
must've fallen asleep on it.

The man's mouth paces, unacquiescent,
going through doors just to slam them.

I jump and the man's
skin comes with me.

Room 312

Everyone should have a place. Like Richard,
I thought mine was inside someone else.

We moved the party.
What a strange place for tea. Clean khakis.

Progress: We dress ourselves kindly.
My check-ins sound like this:

I wake and one hand is tapping the other.
I wake and one hand is dead on the pillow

and when it wakes it will strangle me.
I wake and my foot has been replaced

by my hand. Check — They all look
at my shoe while the next guy

talks about feeling pretty good despite seeing his ex
sleeping downtown on a piece of cardboard.

The next guy talks about 150 pounds later
and not feeling anything for fifteen years.

There is always a next guy.
Only the virtuous one

is allowed to sing the last chorus.
It will be so inspiring. There is no last chorus.

We feel dirty. We're in this forever.
We get up and make the bed.

Self-Compassion

Is it never again 1976
when I was really getting
somewhere with language?

In other words, I wish to pull
the little bent nails from everything
I've banged together.

I would entitle this installation
of surplus commas, *Self-Compassion*,
but who would attend?

After the hardest times,
people will let you know
you were thought *of*.

Tenses are so emotional.
Like when I think about
past and future surgeons.

I slit open
an intriguing envelope
from Sunset Peach,

the hotel where my mother
asked me if she should
call me her son.

Together we did
poor detective work
to find lost worlds.

When people are having
difficult times, I say to them,
It will be night then day

then night again. Because this
is what the world does.
That's all it does.

Something Goes Here

We are learning about
the hole at the centre
of our beings.

It is said the hole
will eventually be filled
with the list we're to make,

filled with our own
well-rested and belovedness
until we no longer yearn

to empty shot after shot
into it. Sometimes people
speak this way and I remember

they have it both
exactly right
and exactly wrong.

I see my list
is as strange and small
as the next fellow's:

sleep
movies
trees

Mine instructs me
to retrieve my warm
writing sweater.

The soft one
with the exquisite hole
below the left clavicle.

The size of some
narrative bit
I don't wish to recall.

I take up the hole as gently
as if it were the final dead pet
from the bottom

of the birdcage of being eleven
and visiting my father
for the last time.

The hole isn't a mouth.
Only an ink-blue opening
I lie down in to listen.

To Thine Own Self

In the Yoga Cancelled Today room
we redistribute thoughts

of incorrect portions. Everything
is another way of family.

Today I am leaving
and the counsel of Polonius

is being unironically expounded.
I take advice how I can get it.

I am told
my face will be missed.

At least
it's really my face now.

Drinking your face off,
sadly apt.

Gentlemen's

Nature,
I also believed
my first suit
would never be replaced.

Sitting here
I'm moving emptily
toward the interior
of things

while the great-out-of-doors
waits for me saying:
Well then I'm broke.
Well then I'm scared.

If I think these thoughts
in many more
public restrooms,
I'll be finished

with believing in anything
but excrement.
Though having passed
hauntingly scented borders

in airports, gas stations
and this recovery centre
with lowered eyes and silence
attendant my idea of men

to the safety
of a personal stall,
I feel evolving.
And what is the job

of an artist anyway,
say if you are a creature like
a shark or a tree
or common bacterium

and there is a tank
or poem
or an idea
about immortality?

Even in an instrument
like that, it sounded
like I was alive,
says the E. coli.

More Reasons

Who's in here
with me?
my amygdala
still sometimes says.

Now all your secrets
have left, you are
unified and dead.
Mary Ruefle.

Who is so cryptic
and really gets it right.
I am a whirlwind
of losses and gains.

When I speak so widely,
don't words seem
too large for the task,
too loosely attached

to the animal?
No animal cares
for more reasons.
For our terrible deeds.

This morning I thought —
so simply and autonomously
it might have tasted
like orange juice —

Someone is finally here!
And it wasn't unlike,
Today you won't struggle
to know. But it was only

myself saying it's time to pack up
again. Though I'm yet unable
to return home. Harbour
to enemies in their brightness

and friends in their equalizing
dark. The day you realize
you can collect the bodies
is a good day. Immediately

I discharge with warm strength
through time to dress
the body in the woods
in a T-shirt. It's the size

of a ten-year-old boy. I once
left it hanging on a nail.
Next to the cracked paddles.
Bound-up sails.

Daily Visit

I am waiting for a man
in white pants
with a soft broom.

The lineup is no shorter
or longer than one
might expect: one.

You keep looking
for your body
inside someone else,

the man had said
on his website.
Wouldn't that be a pretty

serious trespass,
at the very least,
a terrible mistake?

I am lying at the foot
of the Sangre de Cristo
Mountains with my shirt off,

reminding myself
it can take only one night
to desert oneself

and countless to learn
how to return.
It is growing

dark again,
so I would like a drink.
But I am waiting.

For the man
in white pants
and his soft broom.

*

Snow, Night, in the Defunct Lyric of Masculinity

See how snow creates
a large stillness of actual
warmth that answers,
a little, togetherness?

The clear entry of one
single-known thought.
It changes everything
and is enough.

Falling and cold,
it is so good
I stop
ascending.

It's a scale of just.
Love,
not its causes.
Lying naked,

subject to, skinned.
A soft, pink and sweet-smelling
coffin.
And night,

all loosely woven and matte,
with nothing else to do
but withdraw to bed
and decline one's own misuse.

Decline to pluralize
one moment for a fast take
that would too badly subjugate
the really entrancing

cinematography.
Decline even one moment
of what isn't wanted
for there's so much that is.

And on this
allowing of entrance and exit
from the only home
one ever has, and to whom,

I received instruction
from the traumatized dog
who wants in and out,
but on his terms.

And it is his house really,
but on in I come each day
as though it's mine, tromping
over the lace of paw scent.

Exclude is keeping
something out,
preclude is preventing
something from happening,

disclude was to shut apart
but now means
to make known.
Do whatever you need.

To absent oneself.
Without anything to choose,
one doesn't. Consequently,
no table of contents.

The idea of space never changed
since finding oneself
alone in a room, withstanding
one's own nature like a lover.

But space is moving.
It's all tame and then lively,
isn't it?
We ask the animals,

What are you trying to tell me, boy?
then sit around eating their ribs.
I forgot to begin this
by offering gratitude

for my life and body.
I try to accept them every day.
Even when there isn't one
angle from which I don't wither.

Earlier, I did not wish to shave.
I was more prepared
to enshrine
than to remove a single hair.

Himself, he thinks,
withholding the mirrorist.
Pow, he thinks. Two
unreflective spheres, unadorned.

How this relates: I am
forever producing male
identification documents
with my eyes. Going through

a place called "security,"
or when I am found
travelling too fast by pickup
through someone else's state.

I feel scared to let them look
and am excited by their looking.
If I leave with any other
ambivalence it will not be

the rejection of corporeal
imprisonment from which
I hereby revoke my existence,
I bluster.

He takes down *his* thoughts,
his hair,
his trousers,
his buddy.

He, unsolvable, does not desire
an alcoholic beverage.
He would prefer the beverage
of alcoholics, club soda.

The scale of *his* pain.
And if I can enter
this, the golden-throated era
of the hormone

and blow lightly over nature
to receive not only fire
but the endlessly relaxing,
Leave him be, well I shall.

Whoever said truth
involved continuity.
I perform again and again.
I am not a performance.

Nothing Made of Golden Beams

Direct radiation
has scattered

bluely. Where I am
is a dusty library

of coming clean.
Wherein is shelved

an agreement about air:
how much should be allowed

to come between us. Even
at its thinnest we are in it

with our fingers, attempting spring.
This world is so wide open,

it is we who
wear lock and key.

Gesture Is Part of the Identity

This new life isn't all bad.
Sitting in a chair, drinking
from the mug with a chair
on it is so inspiring to me

that instead of saying I want
to say something beautiful,
I will try to *say* something
beautiful. And then the page

goes blank. Then asterisks,
like snowflakes. My brain
is alive, and I remember
it's not decaf.

I am writing this
with the pencil
someone I love left behind
when they left.

It is sexy and has
mysterious green
lettering. This is what I'm
doing with it, okay?

Declivity is a beautiful
word. A thickly wooded
declivity is suggested,
then *proclivity*, followed by

perversity, and I am
inclined to yours,
wondering, why don't
I give up poetry and start

wearing dresses?
My fear arrow assignment
is on Beauty and help me
it's spectacular in here.

The pink dress
you saw for sale
on the side of the road
on the way to the airport,

I don't move in it
like the wind does
but it doesn't matter,
I am wanted in it.

I could say something
beautiful if I only had
until this pencil ran out.
I would be so careful.

Forge

I am drinking coffee
that is nearly too strong
for my own good.
It was ordered up

by my past self.
In the hammering
I feel the deformed
forge god — the only

ugly god — forging
a wiry old man
in the heart of me.
When I speak of him

like this, I am no longer
worried sick about the *him*.
But you, too, are smart
about language's

carefully moving hands
and constant dull
shoulder blades.
I'll not get too into the lyric

of metallurgic workings
but I am unable to easily
burst forth these days.
Or as yet unaccustomed

to the suggestive resonance
of musicality and masculinity.
Perhaps never have I
so somnambulized my small

readership with boundaried
generalizations. But newly,
I wish this life
to always be mine.

Please point me
to a religion with no hope
for union so love for life
draws near for good.

Hawk & Hare

Whenever you say
my name, it sounds
like the sweetest,
most vocative,

masculine singular.
You save it
for the precise moment
you give yourself away.

You want to kneel
so badly. You are dying
to get out in the open
because it matters to you

to tell the truth. You fall apart
in darkness — I open my stitches.
We are descendants
of disgust and prayer

working our divorces
from the sky
to disorganize toward life.
We try to keep to ourselves

the daily falling apart.
We seek what gives us
the slip — we lie in bed
and wiggle for it.

The earth still moves
by the bumpy postal services
of love and sex. You,
who have many impulses:

in each, an actuary.
We practice this position
called Hawk & Hare
and somewhere

in our mission
to unproductively synthesize
and look happily
into each other,

we are so naked,
so troubled in shape,
our bodies become
unrecognizable.

Shazam

Let's right here,
right now, agree
to never again
speak of time.

And speaking of time,
unlike a sonnet, I hope
to be a form that isn't
too late for itself. My own,

little Shazam
that never fails
to recommend you to me,
is such a slim vial.

Let's *really* be alive now.
We can lie in bed
and come up with interesting
pamphlets on our failures.

Cage

My new body
is narrow and dangerous

and in it a man's voice
watches for John Cage's baton

to lift upward to play
not silence

but readiness. Readiness
to let unprepared sounds

drown out
the great orchestration.

Disinhibition

At the worst of it,
and the best,

arousal tucks its knees
behind our own.

When I asked you,
for the duration

of even a birthday candle,
to lie behind me,

it was come what may.
Our hot rod bodies.

As fast as they go,
the gods go faster.

Sad Desire Ad

You are brought to me
in a suit of small mirrors.

You are wearing
my skin

or nothing,
or each other.

You are holding this book
or my breath, or the gaze.

Something Goes Here

I have permanent
editing marks

on my chest
and stomach.

It's a good excuse
to lift my shirt

and have you say
I look sexy

and normal
and alive.

But First, the Paperwork

I am always on the lookout
for smallish men

like me.
One once wrote

a list of things to do
along a nearby river.

The list smells of cologne
and reads, in part,

Go to the bridge
and press its buttons.

I have managed
only the unwritten,

which asks of me,
Press this note

to your face,
breathe deeply

and never again
be in touch.

Swan

A woman falls from a bridge
and a beautiful man

is lifted from the river
with dead tenderness.

It's winter and he's in
someone else's arms now.

The palm at the end
of his hanging arm

is open to the autopsic
light. And maybe you

look out past him
because you need

to keep moving, it's cold,
and the man is heavier

than the woman ever was,
and did you ever even need

to carry her?
Your mind moves

in a flurry. It was
you. You, who stripped

and scotched yourself
of everything for him.

He has only ever
weighed you down.

Your own skeleton breaks
under his slab weight.

What holds you here,
in this whiteness?

What but the attempt
to transform us into something

intimately halfway
between whatever this is

we keep doing
to each other.

Gold Hill

Impossible to take a reading now.
He can't hear a sound for miles.
But ten miles above the house
someone calls him in.

He doesn't answer.
He spends his days
not looking up.
The sky is liquor,

you see, gold.
It could pour
down his throat
if he gave it even a glance.

Infinite and existential,
timeless and finite,
addicted and *what?* he thinks,
connected, they say,

and he defers
rather than disagrees,
to find he can't go home
until he can hear it all.

He fears this, too,
may be bottomless.
He is trying to stand
in the granite of his own

voice. *He*, with his small
bag of bent nails, striking
this new word to the fence,
the dry field beyond it, the mountain

above that. To hold it there.
The hammer slips
through the light, the nail
slips through the light,

the light slips
from him until
there's no matter at all,
nothing's the matter.

He cranks it back
again, his voice
shales
but what is he even saying?

Something about how
she slipped from him
and ran up the mountain
like a shadow.

I'm Always Here, Except When I'm Not

It all continues,
walking into a rainy night
burning the archives

like the Romantics
in the Province of Opposites.
This is about undoing

the projection. It's about
whether this carries on
without us.

At least the small owl
in the woods
is not a barred subject. Well,

it is and it isn't. Regarding
the ability to be here, I have
mysterious instructions

to recite a poem
known well enough
to lift the falling

black curtains.
Who? Secrets,
I feel their hands

at my throat.
I have been trying
to make them go away.

Phew. You are sad
you're away, I think.
It's so wide in there

without me,
saying these words
about the invisible.

Now, I do not wish
to say goodbye but
I've a chest to quiet,

eyes to close,
and the raindrops
are starting to freeze.

Transition

It's this not knowing
when the guest will leave
and you are the guest.

Not quite knowing where
to sit, the couch? Or how
often to clean or cook before

it's more a chore
for your host
who seems to be a horse

with eyes that narrow
in the wide open of your stay.
I've not once mentioned

a higher power and now
here is this horse. Her coat
is the colour of how much

night is required to see
the barely glowing light switch
I speak to from bed.

Please tell me,
where can we go from here?
And look, if I knew

where I left my
light jacket
I'd put it on already.

A man is going crazy
because he has seen
a colour no one else has

but there is no way
to prove it exists
for no one but him.

It is the colour of my jacket,
I'm certain. I'm going to need it.
It's almost spring.

This book was written on land governed and stewarded for generations by the Musqueam, Squamish, Tsleil-Waututh, Songhees, Esquimalt, WSÁNEĆ and Taos Pueblo people.

With love and thanks to: Elizabeth Hayes, Lisa Lewis and Co., my grandmother who is in my eyes now, Melanie Siebert, Anne-Marie Turza, Garth Martens, Tara Lindsay and Boon. At VAMP: Laurie, Michael, Sam, Scott and everyone whose good boots were in that circle. In travels: Amber and Jamie, Isa, Kate Douglas and Co., Elee Kraljii Gardiner, Hamilton, Miranda Pearson, Betsy-Oscar Warland, and Mollie, Jess and Jasmine. And to Rebecca Gagan, Kim Gilmour, Phil Hall, Richie Knight, David Seymour and everyone at icehouse poetry and Goose Lane Editions, the Electronic Garrett, the University of Victoria, Moving Trans History Forward, and friends, family and colleagues who helped me and the book along the way.

Some of these poems first found their homes in the following publications: *After You, A Portrait in Blues Anthology* (England), *Arc Poetry Magazine*, the *Fiddlehead*, *I.D.I.O.T* (Slovenia), *Maisonneuve*, *This Magazine, Times Columnist* and *Vallum*.

This book is indebted to thinking from Eileen Myles' *Snowflake/Different Streets* and Lisa Robertson's *Three Summers*, and to lines from Melanie Siebert's *Deepwater Vee*, Garth Martens' *Prologue for the Age of Consequence* and Anne-Marie Turza's *The Quiet*.

I am grateful for support from the Canada Council and the BC Arts Council.

Ali Blythe's first book of poems, *Twoism*, was released by icehouse poetry to critical acclaim in 2015. The *Malahat Review* praised *Twoism*, remarking that "at the heart of Ali Blythe's courageous debut collection is a bruising search for identity" while the *Bull Calf* hailed *Twoism* as "a potent form of touch." Blythe has been lauded as a "surreal engineer of language" (*Scene*) with "wry observation and a chaotic wit" (*Arc Poetry Magazine*).

Blythe is the winner of the Vallum Award for Poetry, a finalist for the Dorothy Livesay Poetry Prize and a finalist for the Dayne Ogilvie Prize for LGBTQ Emerging Writers from the Writers' Trust of Canada. His poems have been published in literary journals and anthologies in Canada, Germany, Slovenia and England. Blythe lives in Victoria, BC.

photo: Nina LaFlamme